T0368697

BANISH THE BARNACLES

LIVING THE CHRISTIAN LIFE SIMPLY

DEBRA LONGER

WESTBOW
P R E S S®
A DIVISION OF THOMAS NELSON
& ZONDERVAN

WestBow Press books may be ordered through
booksellers or by contacting:

WestBow Press
A Division of Thomas Nelson & Zondervan
1663 Liberty Drive
Bloomington, IN 47403
www.westbowpress.com
844-714-3454

ISBN: 979-8-3850-4559-4 (sc)
ISBN: 979-8-3850-4560-0 (e)

Library of Congress Control Number: 2025903897

Print information available on the last page.

WestBow Press rev. date: 04/07/2025

Contents

Contents

Soli Deo Gloria

All glory to God alone

Preface

I would be the last person to tell you what to do.
It is with a sigh of relief that you can realize that
you don't have to *do* everything you thought you did.

You don't have to *do* every single
thing you were taught to do...
And of course, I am speaking here of your faith...
(Because you do have to brush your
teeth and wear shoes in stores.)

It is the joy of just living simply
in a relationship with God after
shrugging off a heavy burden,
and life becomes so much simpler
and so much more joyful
as you focus on the unique destiny
God designed for you.

I am only sharing some observations, thoughts
and perhaps a couple of suggestions for you to consider.
What you do with them is between you and the Lord.

Simple

PART 1

THE BLIGHT OF BARNACLES

Chapter 1

THE BLIGHT OF BARNACLES

Years ago, I noticed that some churches have rules and expected behaviors not found in Scripture. Folks observed some complicated rituals that I couldn't find supported in the Bible. So, I gave some thought to this and tried to figure out why.

The gospel of Christ is really quite simple. Jesus, a perfect man, suffered and died in our place in order that our sins would be forgiven and we could approach God. The veil of the temple was torn in order to show that, with the death of Jesus, we can access God's forgiveness and can now approach a Holy God! Not because of anything *we* have done or earned, but because of what Jesus accomplished on the cross.

Simple. Profoundly simple. Yet "things" were being attached to that. Why? To please others? To make ourselves feel more holy? To score points with God by what we do? Maybe to better our relationship with God by obeying rules? While I am not against rules, it just seemed wrong to infer something is of God when it is not.

I began to call these things we attach to our faith *barnacles*. Barnacles, in the literal sense, are actually creatures categorized as crustaceans. They secrete a substance that sticks to surfaces and then hardens. Which means, of course, they will attach to the surfaces of boats. I am not a boater, but I did some research on barnacles, because I saw a spiritual application.

Barnacles can cover the submerged part of a boat. While a barnacle, in itself, is not a bad or evil creature, the damage they cause can be harmful! Barnacles affect the performance of the boat including not only the surface but also the engine performance reflected in several ways. In other words, no matter how great and expensive your boat, when it is covered with barnacles it will not perform as advertised.

A barnacle is not like an iceberg. They are not like a chunk of ice ramming through your boat, but rather attachments on the surface. One by one, barnacles won't kill you, but they will affect everything about your boat. Spiritual barnacles will affect everything about your life. The more barnacles we allow in our lives, the less we truly represent God.

So, religious barnacles - where *do* they come from? How have we embraced them and allowed them to be attached to our faith? Often barely noticed.

They can come from:

- habits
- traditions
- culture

- things we are told we must do to be "good Christians"
- things we are supposed to do to be obedient.
- those who make a complete doctrine out of one verse
- things that in themselves may not be bad.

We even take on barnacles based on our own experiences. Of course we mean no disrespect to God! We just use what we think is common sense to add stuff onto the gospel. No matter how good our intentions, we need to stop.

When it comes to walking with God, the barnacles we allow to attach to our faith will damage our walk and misrepresent the truth of who Gods is.

(Just a note: When I say "God"
I am looking at the whole of God here:
Father, Son and Spirit.)

All in all,
barnacles misrepresent God.

They take
the shape of the boat,
but they are not the boat.

Chapter 2

BOTCHING BARNACLES

Beaucoup barnacles on an actual boat can cause the boat to be slowed, which will actually use more fuel. I imagine it would be like driving with 43 sloths attached to your car. It definitely creates drag, which would require more power to overcome and get up to speed. Needing more power translates into using more fuel and putting excess strain on the engine. Consider what would happen if some of the sloths got *into* the engine.

Carrying around barnacle baggage wastes energy. Extra baggage is exhausting! Barnacles can load us down with guilt. We all want to please God and do His will, and taking on barnacles may *seem* like a pretty easy way to do this.

God has created each of us for a specific destiny. A unique path just for us. A believer's life is not "one-size-fits-all". Yet, barnacles can give us an appearance of sameness and even unity.

Your relationship with God is not like a dog show. You don't have to look or act a certain way in order to score points with the judge. You don't have to be better or score higher than everyone else, in order to win approval from God. He made you and loves you just the way you are.

Think about it. We are performance trained from childhood: Say thank you, say you're sorry, smile for the camera, say grace. We wait for the "good girl" or "attaboy" and the applause; the A+ on the essay; things that in themselves are not bad.. They just don't *translate* into a loving relationship with God. He already loves us enough (before we even thought of *doing* anything) to let His perfect Son die in our place.

*We can earn
and deserve things
down here in the world.*

*God's kingdom
operates differently.*

Chapter 3

BARNACLE BAGGAGE

As barnacles remain on the boat and grow, they damage the surface of the boat. Imagine the damage those 43 sloths could do to the paint of a car! The long nails, the teeth, and fighting...to say nothing of sloth scat on the car.

Here is my favorite funny/not funny anecdote, and I apologize for not knowing the author: A man walks into a church in a T shirt, shorts and sandals. The usher stops him and says, "You need to go home, and before you come back, ask the Lord what to wear to church." The man leaves and returns the next week in a T-shirt, shorts and sandals. The usher stopped him and said, "Didn't I tell you to go ask the Lord what to wear to church?" The man replied, "I did. And the Lord said, 'I don't know what they wear. I've never been there.'"

When you carry around all those barnacles (religious encumbrances) you misrepresent God. You have then added your opinions, interpretations and habits *onto* the words of God. So, you begin to live with a list of good, correct and expected behaviors. Each day comes with a list of things to do to be a "good" Christian. You do not want to disappoint God or others, because then you would consider yourself a failure. You continue to work hard for the approval of everyone, including God. But this is the God who does *not* put barnacles on you. The God who loves you and values you just as you *are*.

Are we ever directed in the Word to do *anything* for the approval of others? God guides us into His will for us. This is the destiny He designed for us before we were born.

Do you look for tasks to accomplish each day instead of celebrating each moment with joy? Rather than seeing the shape of the clouds, a small flower almost hidden in the grass, or a squirrel jumping from tree to tree, your mind is on all you think you have to *do*. Suddenly, life is a burden and you miss the simple joys. Jesus said He came to give us abundant life. Why would you choose to miss that?

Yes, we do have responsibilities each day: normal things we need to do. But add religious barnacles onto that, and the weight is heavy indeed.

Barnacles are
attachment to the truth.

But they are not
the truth.

Chapter 4

BARNACLES BLIND

The Pharisees were so busy putting their barnacles on Jesus, they couldn't even see the Son of God in front of them! They believed they were being righteous, but they completely misunderstood the purposes of God. They had no vision to see that Jesus was bringing them into a New Covenant. That's because barnacles blind. Just because you are well-meaning and "religious" doesn't mean you are accurately representing God.

Barnacles are big beams. Jesus made it clear in Matthew 7, when He spoke of motes and beams, or specks and logs, that it is sometimes easier (and less painful) to see the barely noticeable speck in the eye of another, than to deal with the log in our own. Barnacles that require certain behaviors are a log in our vision. But unfortunately, that won't prevent us from trying to dig out a speck in the eye of someone else!

If you allow barnacles to be attached to your faith, you will feel free to hand them out to others. That way, you can make them carry the same barnacle baggage you carry. If they don't have the "right" barnacles, you will judge them either in appearance or actions. Your barnacles will blind you to simply loving and accepting others as God does. God never set us up to judge others. What Jesus was saying is when we don't stay in our own lane, we become blind to our own faults, and we get puffed up faulting others.

We need to look at the barnacles *we* have picked up along the way, and get rid of them, because it's quite another thing to look for them in the lives of others. Judgment, itself, can be a barnacle. When we become more focused on what we *do* rather than who we *are,* we bring that focus onto others, and we will see only what they *do* rather than who they *are.*

It's not up to us to be looking for a barnacle, or two, or three, in the lives of others or in the church up the road. We do see what we see. Yet, instead of judging, we can pray that God will open their eyes to the freedom they are missing in Christ. Our job is to watch over our own lives and see that no barnacles are attached to our walk with the Lord.

*Barnacles cause distraction
from the truth
of God's word,*

*and result in a lack of focus
on what is truly important.*

Chapter 5

BARNACLE BURNOUT

Boat engines generally draw from the water they're in to cool the engine, but barnacles can block the engine's water intake. My understanding is, like a poorly functioning radiator in a car, this can lead to overheating. Since water intake is crucial to the cooling of the engine, the intake must be kept clear to avoid overheating. (I am guessing this is like those sloths covering the front of your car's grill.)

When our barnacles become more valuable than the truth of God's Word, our intake will be blocked too. We will have difficulty hearing God's voice. Life will be out of balance. Spiritual truths will no longer be important.

Barnacles, no matter how much they may seem to make sense, will never contribute to living a Christian life of peace. For example, there are times when we need to consider ourselves first, before running around trying to meet the needs of everyone else.

The thing is, when we are always prioritizing others, and never thinking of our own needs, we are following a recipe for a burnout: running out of energy and suffering exhaustion mentally and physically. But it's all in the name of the Lord, so it's supposed to be OK, isn't it? (No, it's not. It's a barnacle.)

A buzzword nowadays is "self-care," and it has nothing to do with selfishness. If you don't love yourself enough to take care of what *you* need, you will not be capable of ministering to others and encouraging their times of rest. When we take care of ourselves, we are then able to encourage others to value themselves.

When we value times of peace and rest, we are living where we were designed to live. Not because we *have* to or someone *told* us to, but because that is the truth. Jesus made no apologies for getting up early to go be alone with His Father, away from others.

Hearing God's voice is difficult when our lives are out of balance. We need to remember we were created to be in Eden. The further we get from that in our daily lives, the more likely we will burn out. Those who are overachievers and allow themselves to burnout, best not do it in the name of the Lord. We will never burn out doing God's will in our lives. Yes, He will stretch us beyond our comfort zone, but our self-inflicted burnout makes us useless.

*It's hard to hear truth
when you are actively
believing lies.*

PART 2
A Bunch of Barnacles

Chapter 6

A BARNACLE NAMED "SHOULD"

There's a barnacle named "should" as in "I should" or "I shouldn't." Right next to that is a barnacle called "ought." How many times has a *should* caused you to feel pressured to do something while not even considering if it is God's will for *you*? But the obligation of "that's what Christians should do" is too strong to resist. The weight of these obligations is heavy. So, along the way, it leads to stress, failure and eventually burnout.

I'm not talking about light-hearted "shoulds" as in "you should try it," meaning, "I think you'd really like it." If we say, "you should go see it," we mean "it's something I think you'll enjoy." Or, "You should try it- it's delicious." I'm not talking about lighthearted suggestions, where people share what they like with others. Or not even, "I should get up and do the dishes." I'm talking about the *shoulds* of performance regarding our faith.

In my early years as a believer, someone told me, "You should read a chapter of Scripture a day." Well, I did so because I was told it was "the right thing to do" and I wanted to do the "right thing." However, what we *"have to do"* eventually becomes a *chore*. God doesn't want our time with Him to be a chore of something we "should" do.

Of course we need to read the Word of God! But to make up a rule and pass it off as truth from God would seem a bit presumptuous. "Give us this day our daily bread" means more than literal food and literal Bible. It means He is our Source of life!

Beware of these *shoulds* and *oughts*. Nothing provokes a Christian believer into action quicker that being told they "should do this" or "shouldn't do that." Unfortunately, the resulting guilt can also be an effective motivator. But God doesn't guilt us into doing His will. Guilt is not how we have a loving relationship with our Father. Remember, *shoulds* and *oughts* generally rely on performance, not the grace of God. Human rules, however well-intentioned, cannot be passed off as rules from God. That would be like adding to God's word.

Sometimes folks find something that works in their own life and then proceed to make it a rule that everyone should do it. And that's where it starts: the rule from one person (not God) that becomes a *should*. We take on the responsibility to share that weighted *should* with others, thus handing them a barnacle! We make what we believe *we* should do into something *everyone* should do.

We weren't designed for the burden of "should." *Shoulds* and *oughts* change our focus onto what we think we *should* do instead of what God is actually calling us to do, resulting in a waste of time and energy. Debating the pros and cons of "what if I do or what if I don't?" delays decisions and prevents action. Arguing with a barnacle is exhausting!

It is important to understand that we don't need to start *doing* things to earn God's approval. He already loves us! He loved us when He created us! He loved us even before we came to Him through Jesus. He's not going to love us any more by watching us do good things, while we think that we are *earning* His favor or His blessing.

It would seem that after we are saved, we get mixed up between Paul's advice, the Old Testament rules and modern day Pharisees. We forget that we were brought to God by *grace*. So many folks just accept a list of *shoulds* as if doing those will make us even right-er with God.

Most of us have finally understood that we don't need to "clean ourselves up" before coming into a relationship with God. We understand that Jesus did it all, and nothing we do can would make us righteous enough to come into God's Holy presence without the blood of Jesus covering our sins.

But, some may want to **add** to the Spirit led life, by suggesting tasks that would make us appear more righteous or even spiritually mature. Perhaps we want to present a more holy appearance either in the eyes of God or our peers. We know we are saved by the grace of God-not because of anything we can do! Then after we are in relationship with God, we are so excited and thankful, we want to "pay Him back" for all He's done for us! As if we could! And, even if we *could,* there is nothing that would be adequate to compensate for what Jesus did for us!

Now this is not to say that we can sit around every day

eating bonbons saying "Thank you Jesus." I'm not saying don't *thank* Jesus. (Nor am I saying don't eat bonbons.) I *am* saying that resting in relationship with God is not a license for inactivity. Because His Spirit **will** lead us to do things. But, we need to be led by God's Spirit, not pushed by human *shoulds*.

We *will* do things, not because we have to and feel obligated; but because God has whispered them into our hearts. Not because we fear disappointing Him, but because His plan is that we walk in the destiny He created for us.

This makes the motivation an overflow of relationship with God. He guides us to go here or do this, not because we *have* to or someone told us to; but because we chose to listen to God's voice speaking to our hearts. Everything comes from this place: hand in hand with Him releasing His love to others. He guides and leads us into what we say or do.

When God's word says that we should be doers and not just hearers, it does not mean we have to **do things** in order to be obedient to God. It simply means we will hear and **then put into practice** what we have heard from God.

The wavering and inability to make a choice while we evaluate a *should* creates uncertainty in our lives. The result of uncertainty is stress, which is just about the *opposite* of peace. Tension and indecision are never God's will for us! If we truly surrender the reins of our life to Him, we would eliminate a lot of the stress we cause by "trying to do the right thing!"

God gives us free will to choose our destiny, both in day to day life and in eternity. God doesn't place expectations and *shoulds* on us. He loves us enough to give us free will to choose. But sometimes we don't treat each other with that same respect regarding the freedom to choose. Which is why we load others up with expectations and *shoulds*. By not accepting that people can use their God-given gift of free will to choose, we are actually contradicting God's plan.

When a "barnacular should"
takes precedence
over God's will for you,
be careful-

You just might be saying good-bye
to your time and your peace.

Chapter 7

THE BARNACLE OF OBLIGATION

Closely related to the barnacle of "should" is "obligation."
For example, do we feel that showing up every Sunday at
church fulfills an obligation to God? Fulfilling obligations
to the Lord is a sad way to live our lives. Sad in so many
ways. We could never pay God back for what He's done
for us: for redeeming us, for saving us and for forgiving
us. Those are just a few things He freely gives! Not to
mention that trying to "pay Him back" is contradictory
to what grace is. God *gives* us grace. He *gives* us mercy. He
doesn't want us to be obligated to Him. He simply wants
us to accept His gifts freely.

In fact, I wonder if it grieves the Lord when we feel
obligated to show up on Sunday. And if we miss church,
to feel like we've sinned. "Keeping the Sabbath holy" does
not mean you **have** to go to church. Our relationship
with God is that: it's a *relationship*. Obligation has nothing
to do with it. God isn't obligated to love us. He loves us
because that's His character. It is who He is!

We are not obligated to go to church, unless we choose that barnacle of obligation. However, we may *choose* to go. If we believe that the teaching, worship and singing with fellow believers will encourage and strengthen us, we can go if we want to. We are free to make choices about what will build us up, but we certainly need not choose obligation.

Don't get me wrong! People can serve the Lord in many ways, yet still have a life filled with barnacles. I just wonder about the cost for that in their lives and the lives of those around them, both in the time of exhaustion and in the time wasted with questions about decisions and priorities. People serve the Lord with barnacles in their lives every day and may not even be aware because "that's how it's always been done."

*Obligation cheapens
the grace and mercy
of God.*

Chapter 8

THE BARNACLE OF EXPECTATION

We place our expectations on everyone everywhere: cashiers, friends, parents, children, workers. Some expectations are obvious: employers *expect* the employees they hired to do their jobs, and the employees *expect* to be paid. Police *expect* you to obey the laws. Teachers *expect* students to do homework and study.

Expectations aren't wrong in themselves, as some are actually reasonable.

It's when our expectations move into our relationships and spiritual life, (as a way of exerting our will over others) that there is a problem. Consider this: aren't most expectations self-serving?

In fact, aren't many of the expectations we place upon others wanting them to be *just like us?* We want them to do what we want. That would mean they would have to have been raised like us, and to have developed that same common sense we believe we have. To have our morals, our work ethic, our taste in things.

And here's the really unfortunate part: when we have expectations of others, we provide an opportunity for them to be a failure by not living up to our standards. Meaning, without even realizing it, that we are constantly testing others.

Our expectations precede judgment. When others don't meet our expectations, we have no choice but to judge them as *failures*. They failed to meet our expectations! Which suggests we possibly see them as immature, ignorant or even as losers. Then, how do we react? We are either disappointed, hurt, angry or even all three.

Placing our expectations on other people makes us judge and jury, convicting them according to *our* standards or according to what *we* believe is true. We don't have the right to do that. When we become judge and jury it eliminates all possibility of compassion, and blocks the way for mercy and grace. Then we find ourselves stuck in a place outside of God's design for His children.

Face it: expectations do no good, except to provide an opportunity for failure. Our expectations are based upon performance; and people either measure up or they don't. And consider this: don't expectations come from a place of dominance making them a type of control?

"I expect them to be here at 5:00." Does that mean...

- I gave an order and they will let me down if it doesn't happen.
- I will be angry if they don't do what I said.
- My expectation is based upon their performance of my wishes.

31

(Quick thought: "If you're here by 5, we won't be late.")

The more harshly we express our expectations, the greater the *potential for failure* we provide for others. Also, the *more* expectations we place upon others, the more the opportunities for failure. *And* the greater the opportunity for our disappointment in them and/or anger towards them. Even if we LOWER our expectations, we would still have expectations.

How about when *you* fail the expectations of others? When that happens to you, it is legit for you to draw a boundary. You are free to *not* interact with the expectations of others. Sometimes no response is the best response. Our life goal is to do *God's* will, not the will of *others*.

If you *always* do something people are going to simply expect you to continue doing it. We are creatures of habit and that's how expectations get started. Again, some are not all bad. It just doesn't leave much room for change or spontaneity.

Placing expectations on the people around us, will find us facing a fair amount of disappointment. If instead, we adopt an attitude of acceptance by recognizing that humans aren't perfect, we will see less drama and more peace in our lives.

The reason expectation is such a big barnacle to consider is that we have to look at it two ways. First, when we put our expectations on others we're putting a barnacle on *them*. And the second part is that other people will put their expectations on *us* handing *us* a barnacle. Whether it's what they think your career should be, what church you should go to or what you should do, we need to be aware. So whether we're "barnacle-izing" or it's being done to us, our eyes need to be open.

God is always the Answer. We need to realize there is only One who will never disappoint us! And Who will never be disappointed *in* us! God is the perfect example of relationship. He always loves with unconditional love and unlimited forgiveness. He always accepts us for who we are and where we are right now. Which is to say He completely understands our humanity. He never places expectations on us since He already knows what we will do. God knows us too well!

God has explained life in balance in so many ways. And we selfishly mess that up in so many ways! Jesus didn't come to judge but to point the way to His Father. We instead often place a stumbling block of judgment upon others who fail to meet our standards.

Expectations are not the same as hope. Hope is about *you*. Whereas expectation is about *others*. Hope you can own in yourself. Expectation depends upon others. Expectations are a dead end: pass or fail. Hope *remains*.

*When we depend upon others
for fulfillment in any way,
we place our
satisfaction and happiness
in the hands of others.*

*And we already know humans
are not perfect.
That's why we hope in God.*

Chapter 9

BARNACLE BITS

THE BARNACLE OF IMPORTANCE

There's a barnacle based on the fact that some people are considered more important than others in God's Kingdom. Yet, there's that old adage: "the floor is level at the foot of the cross." Which means everybody comes to Jesus the same way. Nobody's more important. We are all equally loved by God. He doesn't love anybody more than others. And it's the same way after you start walking with God and you come into relationship with Him. Nobody's more important than you. Some people are more visible in their ministries, perhaps, but they're not more important to God. They're not more loved by God. And we do sometimes see this in churches where some people are just considered more valued than others. That's not true, and it flies in the face of who God is: a loving Father who loves all His children equally.

No one's prayers are heard louder than yours. No one

has a greater standing with God than you. You *are* that important!

Here's a few more barnacles I have experienced. Plus, I am sure you have a few barnacle stories of your own! I am sharing from my experience, and from the standpoint of the freedom I now have.

CRACKER CRITICISM

- I was criticized (harshly) from someone who did not accept Communion with Matzo crackers and grape juice. It seems she felt that the only right way was with real wine and "wafers." We are products of our upbringing unless we come to understand otherwise.

- Many years ago, a bunch of us celebrated communion with orange juice and graham crackers at a campfire. We were on a retreat sitting around the campfire talking about the Lord and thought it was too bad we didn't bring grape juice and crackers. But we wanted to acknowledge the sacrifice of Jesus. So we just used what we had. It's kind of like singing if you don't have a professional voice. You can still make a joyful noise. God looks at the heart.

FREEZE PRAYER

- I was once rebuked for moving during prayer. (This was as an adult.) At first I thought it was a joke. (It was not.) I wonder: if we "pray without ceasing" yet didn't move while in prayer, wouldn't we just have to stand still all day while we pray?

VERY PRIVATE DEVOTIONS: NO CHILDREN ALLOWED

- Years ago, I saw someone interrupted by a child during his "private devotions." He was angry to be interrupted. I don't see that "devotions" are so private that God wants children excluded. Rather, this could be a teaching moment, about our loving God who always welcomes children.
- Just a thought: getting up early to spend time with God (before anyone else is up) worked for Jesus.

"A REAL CHURCH"

- I know there are some folks who will not go to church when it is held outside in the summer, since that is "not a real church." Was the "Sermon on the Mount" invalid, being outside?

"A-CHAPTER-A-DAY"

- I've mentioned that I was told years ago that Christian believers *must* read one chapter of the Bible every day. Nothing wrong with that. Except it's a barnacle. Reading God's Word is wonderful. The more you read the more you will know His Word, and the more you can keep it in your heart. But, A-Chapter-A-Day is not a law. It's not some kind of task from God. Read when you can, as often as you can. A verse or two or whatever God impresses upon your heart! No requirement, but certainly there are benefits. Choose because you want to, not because someone said you have to.

When we make rules for God, thinking we are doing Him a favor, it's time to get back to the simplicity of the gospel. In themselves, some ideas might be good advice, but when we teach that God requires them or that they are in Scripture, they are barnacles.

Advice is one thing.

Telling others to
obey our ideas to please God
is quite another.

PART 3

BARNACLE BREAKAWAY

Chapter 10

BREAKING AWAY FROM BARNACLES

Why get rid of barnacles? Because barnacles in our lives are man-made rules and expectations and based upon performance: not on the grace and mercy God gives us. We grow up in a performance based world. We earn cookies, allowances, trophies, awards and applause. We earn by performance. Who rewards us for who we *are*? Do we *need* to be rewarded for who we are?

God's kingdom is very different. He loves us because He is God and He created every cell in every body. He provided a way for us to access Him through Jesus who is the Way, the Truth and The Life. So simple that many folks can't believe it or accept it. Or if they do, they then go beyond this to try to do good religious stuff to earn more of His love. A waste of time and energy. God's love is constant: He will never love you more and He will never love you less. That's one of the wonderful things about God: He never changes, which makes Him a constant in an always changing world.

Adding barnacles to our faith just shows that we don't trust God for who He is. That we don't believe His word that says He has already become our "wisdom, righteousness, holiness and redemption." (I Cor. 1:30) Remember, religious barnacles may not be bad in themselves, but become cumbersome when attached to the Truth.

What should we get rid of? Anything that isn't of God. I know that's a pretty loose definition to consider. First, remember that we can't make a doctrine out of just one verse. This is a common way of attaching barnacles to your faith. People do it. Churches do it.

So if our considered barnacle is created by a one verse quote-it's most likely a man-made rule, and therefore a barnacle. Look carefully: is it based on truth or is it tradition, culture or opinion? Examine each barnacle in the light of the whole of God's word, and ask Him how *you* should handle it.

Whatever makes us believe we will be scoring points with God is a barnacle. Nothing we do will make Him love us more. And we will never convince Him we are now "worthy" of His love or grace. If we could earn points with God to prove we are worthy, then the death of Jesus would have been for nothing.

In the book of Acts, the Bereans were commended for "they received the word with great eagerness, examining the Scriptures daily to see whether these things were so." (Acts 17:11 NASB) It is a good thing to check what you are being told to see if it lines up with Scripture!

- If you hear: "It's the way it's always been done," ask, "Why?"
- If the answer is "Because it's in our church by-laws, or what our church founder said or because I said so..." then ask for *all* the the Biblical references.
- After that you may want to ask the Lord if this is where He wants you to be..

*Jesus never did anything
because it was His religious duty.*

*Everything He did
was from love,
to reveal His Father.*

Chapter 11

BARNACLE BATH: MAINTENANCE

Our lives need regular cleaning and inspection for religious barnacles. This keeps *you* in good working order. Barnacles can become our comfort zone: things we just do because we always have. Habits that we barely notice. Good religious things that may seem to make sense.

Note that we are advised in Psalm 139 to ask God to search us. God knows our thoughts before we even speak them as words. That makes Him the perfect Person to expose the barnacles we have allowed into our lives. When we put ourselves in His hands, and let Him lead us.

Fun fact: boaters are encouraged to keep their boat out of the water when not in use, as barnacles need moisture to survive. We need to spend time apart from the world... sometimes just alone in the presence of God. If we don't step away from the craziness of the world, we won't even be able to hear God's voice. The world is loud. God speaks in the quiet when we can listen.

Be committed to the *truth*. Do not be committed to

religious rules. Jesus made many points about those who make religious rules more important than God. Again, not all rules are wrong. We do have responsibilities and things we need to do. We *should* do the dishes or we *ought* to run to the store. But we are not talking about adulting here. We are talking about simply walking with God according to His truth. Barnacles are only wrong when they are being paraded as God-given.

There is only one mediator between God and mankind, and that is Jesus. We need to protect our lives to be sure nothing comes between us and God. People can help you and counsel you, but they are not God. They can speak words from God. But it is up to *you* to check out what they say to see if it lines up with God's Word.

Keeping our lives barnacle-free will simplify our lives and keep us in line with our God-given destiny.

Jesus spoke about
rivers of living water.
And we need that
in our lives
to keep fresh,

and to keep our faith
simple and pure.

Chapter 12

BARNACLE-FREE LIFE

So what other barnacles am I talking about? Here's an example. Let's just say your Mom used to tell you that you have to wear good clothes to God's house on Sunday as a sign of respect. Nothing *wrong* with that. But with Christian believers, God lives in us and He never leaves us. His home is within us.

So, truth is, our respect and reverence for God is how we live our lives every moment of every day. Not just on Sunday. God sees us in our pajamas. And when we wear our old jeans, He doesn't leave us. He loves us no matter what we wear. God is not stressed out about our appearance. Nor is He more pleased with our "good clothes." Now, as adults, why act differently on Sunday?

Living simply without the weight of obligation and other barnacles is not an excuse for laziness. It is giving you the freedom to hear God's voice without interference. It is living with the freedom to understand that there is no other mediator besides Jesus, and you are able to connect directly to God and hear His voice.

When I look back over my life, I realize that I permitted a lot of things in my life without question. Because there's actually social barnacles as well as religious barnacles that we accept in our lives without question. And if we just take the time to ask "why," sometimes there's a really good reason *why* that needs to be done. And other times there's simply no good reason. I'm sure if you look back you can also see things that you allowed in your life without question. As if we're programmed robots; as if we have no brain to look at things or question them to understand. There's a reason God gave us brains. There's a reason we aren't robots, and it's OK to want to understand why and then determine if it's God's will for us.

- **Refuse to accept the barnacles handed out by others.** You are free in Christ. Free to be uniquely you and walk in the specific destiny He has designed for you. When others want you to be like them, walk away, because you are not called to be like anyone!
- **Use caution with those who make a doctrine by taking one verse out of context.** God's will for us is in the entirety of Scripture. His love is a theme throughout His word. The more you know God and walk in His Spirit, the easier it will be to recognize a barnacle when it shows up.

OK, so let's summarize. The things we attach onto our faith for whatever reason, do not bring us closer to the Lord. Instead, they present almost a hypocrisy of righteousness, as if it's something we hide behind. These are things that we might use to replace the actual presence of God in our lives.

In other words, we have placed a mask around our lives, which is pretty much what barnacles do to a boat. While we are looking at simplicity, consider how complicated concepts do not clearly represent our faith. God is actually very specific, and has made it easy for us to connect with Him! God has spelled out how we approach Him: through Jesus, who is the Way, the Truth and the Life. That's all.

It grieves me that some make connecting with God more difficult than it is. When people present their own rules and ideas in place of the simplicity of who God is, they actually construct a barrier to approaching God.

►**Important fact:** Barnacles can't grow in *fresh* water. Keeping your life clearly focused on God: who He is and who you are in Christ and will keep your life in balance.

Fun Fact:

A boater can use

a power washer to keep

the surface of the boat barnacle-free.

Power washer!

We have access to

all the cleansing Power we need!

How can I keep things simpler?

_____

_____

_____

_____

_____

_____

_____

_____

_____

_____

_____

_____

_____

_____

_____

_____

_____

_____

_____

_____

_____

_____

How can I keep this simpler?

What "barnacle" can I let go of?

_____

_____

_____

_____

_____

_____

_____

_____

_____

_____

_____

_____

_____

_____

_____

_____

_____

_____

_____

_____

_____

What Scripture do I need to look into in a deeper way?

_____

_____

_____

_____

_____

_____

_____

_____

_____

_____

_____

_____

_____

_____

_____

_____

_____

_____

_____

What am I hanging onto with no good reason?

_____

_____

_____

_____

_____

_____

_____

_____

_____

_____

_____

_____

_____

_____

_____

_____

_____

_____

_____

_____

Am I ready...?

_____

_____

_____

_____

_____

_____

_____

_____

_____

_____

_____

_____

_____

_____

_____

_____

_____

_____

_____

_____

_____

_____

Printed in the United States
by Baker & Taylor Publisher Services